THE
Scripture
Way of
Salvation

THE
Scripture Way of Salvation

Sermons by
John Wesley

Introduction by
Robert E. Coleman

The Scripture Way
of Salvation
Sermons by John Wesley
Edited with an introduction
by Robert E. Coleman

Used by Permission
© 1994
Billy Graham Center

Published by
The Institute of Evangelism
Billy Graham Center
Wheaton, Illinois

ISBN Number 1-879089-17-3

Printed in the United States of America

Contents

Introduction

Few persons have ever lived who exerted more positive influence on their time than John Wesley. His prodigious life and work, spanning most of the Eighteenth Century, epitomized and gave direction to an evangelical revival that changed the face of England.

Born at Epworth, June 17, 1703, he was the second surviving son of Samuel and Susanna Wesley, and the fifteenth of nineteen children. In the Anglican vicar's home where he grew up, he learned early the importance of sound doctrine and vigorous piety.

At the age of ten, John went to London to attend the Charterhouse School, and seven years later, he entered Christ Church College, Oxford. After graduation he offered himself to become a priest of the Church of England, and was ordained a deacon in 1725. For a while he assisted his father in pastoral work, but meeting with meager success, he returned to his scholarly pursuits at the University, where he had been made a teaching fellow at Lincoln College.

Here Wesley joined his brother, Charles, along with a few other students, in a closely knit fellowship of earnest souls seeking God's will. The group met regularly for study and worship, practiced fasting twice a week, and engaged themselves in a number of benevolent services to the poor. Because of their vigorous discipline they were dubbed in derision "The Holy Club" or "Methodists."

Following his father's death in 1735, John accepted an appointment as a missionary to the colonists and Indians in Georgia. However, his strict adherence to order did not set well with the more easy-going frontiersmen of the new world. A courtship rejection by one of the ladies of the colony added to his difficulties. Finally, after nearly two years of frustration, the broken Wesley returned to England. Typifying his anguish, on shipboard he wrote in his *Journal,* "I went to America to convert the Indians; but O! Who shall convert me?"[1]

Back in London, his longing for spiritual reality eventually led to a little Moravian prayer meeting on Aldersgate Street. There on May 24, 1738, about a quarter before nine, while a layman was reading from Luther's Preface to the Book of Romans, "describing the change which God works in the heart through faith in Christ," Wesley laid hold on the promise of grace, and received assurance that he was delivered from the law of sin and death.[2] This experience kindled a fire in his life which was to set a nation aflame.

England was in desperate circumstances. Centuries of turmoil had left the people bitter and restless. Poverty was everywhere. Society reeked with moral decay. Making the situation

---

[1] John Wesley, written in his *Journal,* Tuesday, January 24, 1738, *The Heart of John Wesley's Journal* (New Canaan, CT: Keats Publishing, 1979), p. 29.

[2] John Wesley, *Journal,* May 24, 1738, *Ibid,* p. 43.

more tragic, the apathetic, established church was completely discredited and out of touch with the working masses.

Into this generation of despair, seething on the verge of revolution, John Wesley began to herald a Gospel of free and full salvation—a deliverance which any person can know through simple faith in the finished work of Jesus Christ. Sophisticated churchmen closed their doors to his preaching. But Wesley, seeing all the world as his parish, following the example of George Whitfield, "submitted to be more vile," and began to proclaim in the streets and fields the glad tiding of salvation.[3]

Soon the soft-spoken Oxford don in clerical garb, standing scarcely five feet four inches tall, with his long, silken hair blowing in the wind, became a familiar sight across the land. Multitudes were arrested by his message, especially the poor, the outcasts of society, and those disenchanted with the cold religious institutions of the day.

For fifty years Wesley carried his ministry to the people. Hazardous conditions never deterred him from his mission to reform the nation and to spread Scriptural holiness over the land. It is estimated that he traveled 250,000 miles on horseback. During this period he preached 42,000 sermons, an average of more than 15 a week. Still, shortly before his death on March 2, 1791, his eyes dim, his right hand

---

[3] John Wesley, *Journal*, April 2, 1739, *Ibid.*, p. 47.

shaking with a lingering fever almost every day, he wrote in his *Journal*: "Blessed be God, I do not slack my labor."[4]

Part of his energy was given to reading and study, particularly the Bible which he revered as the inerrant Word of God. Out of this came a profusion of writings on a wide variety of subjects, including Gospel tracts, letters, appeals, hymns, textbooks, histories, Bible commentaries, and a well-kept personal journal.

It was in his written sermons, however, that his message comes through most fully. Though most of the illustration material was edited out before publication, the keen reasoning of his theology cannot be missed. Whatever the theme, at its heart will be seen the need and provision for heart purity. "Our main doctrines," wrote Wesley, "which include all the rest are repentance, faith and holiness. The first of these we account, as it were, the porch of religion; the next, the door; the third, religion itself."[5]

The three sermons reproduced in this book typify this preaching—the kind of preaching that uncovers the depths of sin while exalting the heights of redeeming grace. The first sermon is a message on Ephesians 2:8. Its genesis goes back to Wesley's early ministry, probably the substance being preached on May 14, ten days before his conversion. When proclaimed

---

[4] John Wesley, *Journal*, January 17, 1790, *Ibid.*, p. 481.
[5] Letter to Thomas Church, written June 17, 1746, in *The Letters of the Reverend John Wesley, A.M.*, ed. by John Telford, II (London: The Epworth Press, 1931), p. 268.

again on June 11, at Oxford, now eighteen days after his conversion at Aldersgate, it must have had a different ring. The manifesto, "Salvation by Faith," announced a new day in religion. Apparently it was one of Wesley's favorites, for it was placed first in his collection of sermons and there are numerous references to it throughout his *Journal*, up to 1760. Sometime after this, the sermon was entirely rewritten, and published in 1765 as "The Scripture Way of Salvation."

The revised message gives more attention to the place of prevenient grace in God's saving work, while also treating more adequately his position on faith and sanctification. The concise exposition affords an excellent overview of basic Wesleyan thought. From this standpoint, one eminent scholar has said that the sermon "is of more practical value than all the sermons put together.[6] Be that as it may, it summarizes great truth, and befitting its evangelist-author, leaves one with a challenge for decision. The instructions of the 1766 *Minutes*, that this message be distributed to all Methodist Societies, has lost none of its urgency in the subsequent more than two hundred years.

The second sermon, "The Circumcision of the Heart," again one of Wesley's earliest preserved discourses, was preached first at Oxford at St. Mary's Oxford on New Year's Day, 1733. It reflects the aspirations of that little group of

---

[6] Dr. J.A. Beet, *London Quarterly Review*, January, 1920, as quoted in Edward H. Sugden, *Wesley's Standard Sermons*, II (London: The Epworth Press, 1968), p. 443.

earnest souls in the University banded together to seek the holy life. Delivered more than five years before Wesley's heartwarming experience at Aldersgate, the sermon describes his concept of holiness worked out intellectually by honestly searching the Scriptures. Though later his views of sanctification were given more refinement, writing to a friend in May of 1765, he said: "This sermon...contains all that I now teach concerning salvation from all sin, and loving God with an undivided heart."[7] Interestingly, when the message was published in his *Second Volume of Sermons* in 1748, Wesley mentions in a footnote that he had added to the original manuscript a more complete definition of saving faith as he had come to experience it in 1738.[8]

The selection concludes with his message, "The Repentance of Believers," written on April 24, 1767, and published in pamphlet form

---

[7] Letter to John Newton, written at Londonberry, May 14, 1765, in Telford, *Letters*, IV, p. 299. An entry in his *Journal*, September 1, 1778, also is significant. He says: "I know not that I can write a better sermon on the circumcision of the heart than I did five and forty years ago, than I did then, and may know a little more History or Natural Philosophy than I did; but I am not sensible that this has made any essential addition to my knowledge in Divinity. Forty years ago I knew and preached every Christian doctrine which I preach now," in *The Works of John Wesley*, 1872 Edition, IV, reproduction (Grand Rapids: Zondervan Publishing House), p. 1350. It is interesting that the later reference to forty years, as distinguished from the former mention of forty-five years, would go back to 1738, when Wesley personally received by faith the consciousness of a new heart.

[8] Sugden, *Wesley's Standard Sermons*," I., *op. cit.*, p. 265.

the following year. It was included in the 1771 edition of his *Works* to further elucidate his message, "On Sin in Believers" (1763). Getting at the true spirituality, the sermon stresses the necessity of dealing with man's self-nature contrary to the mind of Christ. Though not as definitive as his *Plain Account on Christian Perfection* (1766), it underscores the all sufficiency of God's grace enabling one to live under the complete lordship of the King, while showing how repentance and faith answer each other. No one can read this message without being moved. To me it is the most searching of all Wesley's preaching.

These sermons are reprinted unabridged as published in the 1771 Edition of Wesley's *Works*. At a time when many spokesmen of the church seem intent upon entertaining our self-centered generation, lest people take offense, we would do well to listen again to the probing voice of John Wesley. One may take exception to his views, but there can be no dispute that under such preaching forces of righteousness were set in motion that still have reverberations across the earth.

Robert E. Coleman

1
The Scripture Way of Salvation

Ye are saved through faith. - Eph. 2:8

Nothing can be more intricate, complex, and hard to be understood, than religion, as it has been often described. And this is not only true concerning the religion of the Heathens, even many of the wisest of them, but concerning the religion of those also who were, in some sense, Christians; yea, and men of great name in the Christian world; men who seemed to be pillars thereof. Yet how easy to be understood, how plain and simple a thing, is the genuine religion of Jesus Christ; provided only that we take it in its native form, just as it is described in the oracles of God! It is exactly suited, by the wise Creator and Governor of the world, to the weak understanding and narrow capacity of man in his present state. How observable is this, both with regard to the end it proposes, and the means to attain that end! The end is, in one word, salvation; the means to attain it, faith.

It is easily discerned, that these two little words, I mean faith and salvation, include the substance of all the Bible, the marrow, as it were, of the whole Scripture. So much the more should we take all possible care to avoid all mistake concerning them, and to form a true and accurate judgment concerning both the one and the other.

Let us then seriously inquire.

I.   WHAT IS SALVATION?
II. WHAT IS THAT FAITH WHEREBY
     WE ARE SAVED? AND,
III. HOW ARE WE SAVED BY IT?

I. And, first, let us inquire. What is salvation? The salvation which is here spoken of is not what is frequently understood by that word, the going to heaven, eternal happiness. It is not the soul's going to paradise, termed by our Lord, 'Abraham's bosom.' It is not a blessing which lies on the other side of death; or, as we usually speak, in the other world. The very words of the text itself put this beyond all question: 'Ye *are saved*': It is not something at a distance; it is a present thing; a blessing which, through the free mercy of God, ye are now in possession of. Nay, the words may be rendered, and that with equal propriety, 'Ye *have been saved*': so that the salvation which is here spoken of might be extended to the entire work of God, from the first dawning of grace in the soul, till it is consummated in glory.

If we take this in its utmost extent, it will include all that is wrought in the soul by what is frequently termed 'natural conscience,' but more properly, 'preventing grace'; all the drawings of the Father—the desires after God, which, if we yield to them, increase more and more; all that light wherewith the Son of God 'enlighteneth every one that cometh into the world'—showing every man 'to do justly, to love mercy, and to walk humbly with his God'; all the convictions which His Spirit, from time to time, works in every child of man—although it is true, the generality of men stifle them as soon as possible, and after a while forget, or at least deny, that they ever had them at all.

But we are at present concerned only with that salvation which the Apostle is directly speaking of. And this consists of two great parts, justification and sanctification.

Justification is another word for pardon. It is the forgiveness of all our sins; and, what is necessarily implied therein, our acceptance with God. The price whereby this hath been procured for us (commonly termed 'the meritorious cause of our justification'), is the blood and righteousness of Christ; or, to express it a little more clearly, all that Christ hath done and suffered for us, till He 'poured out His soul for the transgressors.' The immediate effects of justification are, the peace of God, a 'peace that passeth all understanding,' and a 'rejoicing in hope of the glory of God' 'with joy unspeakable and full of glory.'

And at the same time that we are justified, yea, in that very moment, sanctification begins. In that instant we are born again, born from above, born of the Spirit; there is a *real* as well as a *relative* charge. We are inwardly renewed by the power of God. We feel 'the love of God shed abroad in our heart by the Holy Ghost which is given unto us'; producing love to all mankind, and more especially to the children of God; expelling the love of the world, the love of pleasure, of ease, of honour, of money, together with pride, anger, self-will, and every other evil temper; in a word, changing the earthly, sensual devilish mind,' into the mind which was in Christ Jesus.'

How naturally do those who experience such a change imagine that all sin is gone; that it is utterly rooted out of their heart, and has no more any place therein! How easily do they draw that inference. 'I *feel* no sin; therefore, I *have* none; it does not *stir*; therefore, it does not *exist*; it has no *motion*; therefore, it has no *being!*'

But it is seldom long before they are undeceived, finding sin was only suspended, not destroyed. Temptations return, and sin revives; showing it was but stunned before, not dead. They now feel two principles in themselves, plainly contrary to each other; 'the flesh lusting against the Spirit'; nature opposing the grace of God. They cannot deny, that although they still feel power to believe in Christ, and to love God; and although His 'Spirit' still 'witnesses with their spirits, that they are children of God'; yet they feel in themselves sometimes pride or self-will, sometimes anger or unbelief. They find one or more of these frequently *stirring* in their heart, though not *conquering*; yea, perhaps, 'thrusting sore at them that they may fall'; but the Lord is their help.

How exactly did Macarius, fourteen hundred years ago, describe the present experience of the children of God; 'The unskillful,' or unexperienced, 'when grace operates, presently imagine they have no more sin. Whereas they that have discretion cannot deny, that even we who have the grace of God may be molested again. For we have often had instances of some among the brethren, who have experienced such grace as to affirm that they had no sin in them; and yet, after all, when they thought themselves entirely freed from it, the corruption that lurked within was stirred up anew, and they were well nigh burned up.'

From the time of our being born again, the gradual work of sanctification takes place. We are enabled 'by the Spirit' to 'mortify the deeds of the body,' of our evil nature; and as we are more and more dead to sin, we are more and more alive to God. We go on from grace to grace, while we are careful to 'abstain from all appearance of evil,' and are 'zealous of good works,' as we have opportunity, doing good to all men; while we walk in all His ordinances blameless, therein worshipping Him in spirit and truth; while we take up our cross, and deny ourselves every pleasure that does not lead us to God.

It is thus that we wait for entire sanctification; for a full salvation from all our sins—from pride, self-will, anger, unbelief; or, as the Apostle expresses it, 'go on unto perfection.'

But what is perfection: The word has various senses; here it means perfect love. It is love excluding sin; love filling the heart, taking up the whole capacity of the soul. It is love 'rejoicing evermore, praying without ceasing, in everything giving thanks.'

II. But what is that faith through which we are saved? This is the second point to be considered.

Faith, in general, is defined by the Apostle πραγματωγ ελεγχοσ ου βλεπομενων—an *evidence,* a divine *evidence and conviction* (the word means both) *of things not seen*; not visible, not perceivable either by sight, or by any other of the external senses. It implies both a supernatural *evidence* of God, and of the things of God; a kind of spiritual *light* exhibited to the soul, and a supernatural *sight* or perception thereof. Accordingly, the Scripture speaks of God's giving sometimes light, sometimes a power of discerning it. So St. Paul: 'God, who commanded light to shine out of darkness, hath shined in our hearts, to give us the light of the knowledge of the glory of God in the face of Jesus Christ.' And elsewhere the same Apostle speaks of 'the eyes of' our 'understanding being opened.' By this two-fold operation of the Holy Spirit, having the eyes of our soul both *opened and enlightened*, we see the things which the natural 'eye hath not seen, neither ear heard.' We have a prospect of the invisible things of God; we see the *spiritual world*, which is all round about us, and yet no more discerned by our natural faculties than if it had no being. And we see the *eternal world*; piercing through the veil which hangs between time and eternity. Clouds and darkness then rest upon it no more, but we already see the glory which shall be revealed.Taking the word in a more particular sense, faith is a divine *evidence* and *conviction* not only that 'God was in Christ, reconciling the world unto Himself,' but also that, Christ loved me, and gave Himself for *me*. It is by this faith (whether we term it the *essence*, or rather a *property* thereof) that we *receive Christ*; that we receive Him in all His offices, as our Prophet, Priest, and King. It is by this that He is 'made of God unto us wisdom, and righteousness, and sanctification, and redemption.'

But is this the *faith of assurance, or faith of adherence?*' The Scripture mentions no such distinction. The Apostle says, 'There is one faith, and one hope of our calling'; one Christian, saving faith; 'as there is one Lord,' in whom we believe, and 'one God and Father of us all.' And it is certain, this faith necessarily implies an *assurance* (which is here only another word for *evidence*, it being hard to tell the difference between them) that Christ loved me, and gave Himself for me. For 'he that believeth' with the true living faith 'hath the witness in himself'; 'the Spirit witnesseth with his spirit that he is a child of God.' 'Because he is a son, God hath sent forth the Spirit of His Son into his heart, crying, Abba, Father'; giving him an assurance that he is so, and a childlike confidence in Him. But let it be observed, that, in the very nature of the thing, the assurance goes before the confidence. For a man cannot have a childlike confidence in God till he knows he is a child of God. Therefore, confidence, trust, reliance, adherence, or whatever else it be called, is not the first, as some have supposed, but the second, branch or act of faith.

It is by this faith we are saved, justified, and sanctified; taking that word in its highest sense. But how are we justified and sanctified by faith? This is our third head of inquiry. And this being the main point in question, and a point of no ordinary importance, it will not be improper to give it more distinct and particular consideration.

III. And, first, how are we justified by faith? In what sense is this to be understood? I answer. Faith is the condition, and the only condition, of justification. It is the *condition*; none is justified but he that believes; without faith no man is justified. And it is the *only condition*; this alone is sufficient for justification. Every one that believes is justified, whatever else he has or has not. In other words: no man is justified till he believes; every man when he believes is justified.

'But does not God command us to repent also? Yea, and to "bring forth fruits meet for repentance"—to cease, for instance, from doing evil, and learn to do well? And is not both the one and the other of the utmost necessity, insomuch that if we willingly neglect either, we cannot reasonably expect to be justified at all? But if this be so, how can it be said that faith is the only condition of justification?'

God does undoubtedly command us both to repent, and to bring forth fruits meet for repentance; which if we willingly neglect, we cannot reasonably expect to be justified at all; therefore both repentance, and fruits meet for repentance, are, in some sense, necessary to justification. But they are not necessary in the *same sense* with faith, nor in the *same degree*. Not in the *same degree*: for those fruits are only necessary *conditionally*; if there be time and opportunity for them. Otherwise a man may be justified without them, as was the *thief* upon the cross (if we may call him so; for a late writer has discovered that he was not thief, but a very honest and respectable person!); but he cannot be justified without faith; this is impossible. Likewise, let a man have ever so much repentance, or ever so many of the fruits meet for repentance, yet all this does not at all avail; he is not justified till he believes. But the moment he believes, with or without those fruits, yea, with more or less repentance, he is justified.— Not in the *same sense*; for repentance and its fruits are only *remotely* necessary; necessary in order to faith; whereas faith is *immediately* and *directly* necessary to justification. It remains, that faith is the only condition which *immediately* and *proximately* necessary to justification.

'But do you believe we are sanctified by faith? We know you believe that we are justified by faith; but do not you believe, and accordingly teach, that we are sanctified by our works?' So it has been roundly and vehemently affirmed for these five-and-twenty years; but I have constantly declared just the contrary; and that in all manner of ways I have continually testified in private and in public, that we are sanctified as well as justified by faith. And indeed the one of those great truths does exceedingly illustrate the other. Exactly as we are justified by faith, so are we sanctified by faith. Faith is the condition, and the only condition, of sanctification, exactly as it is of justification. It is the *condition*; none is sanctified but he that believes; without faith no man is sanctified. And it is the *only condition*; this alone is sufficient for sanctification. Every one that believes is sanctified, whatever else he has or has not. In other words, no man is sanctified till he believes; every man when he believes is sanctified.

'But is there not repentance consequent upon, as well as a repentance previous to, justification? And is it not incumbent on all that are justified to be "zealous of good works"? Yea, are not these so necessary, that if a man willingly neglect them he cannot reasonably expect that he shall ever be sanctified in the full sense; that is, perfected in love? Nay, can he grow at all in grace, in the loving knowledge of our Lord Jesus Christ? Yea, can he retain the grace which God has already given him? Can he continue in the faith which he has received, or in the favour of God? Do not you yourself allow all this, and continually assert it? But, if this be so, how can it be said that faith is the only condition of sanctification?'

I do allow all this, and continually maintain it as the truth of God. I allow there is a repentance consequent upon, as well as a repentance previous to, justification. It is incumbent on all that are justified to be zealous of good works. And these are so necessary, that if a man willingly neglect them, he cannot reasonably expect that he shall ever be sanctified; he cannot grow in grace, in the image of God, the mind which was in Christ Jesus; nay, he cannot retain the grace he has received; he cannot continue in faith, or in the favour of God.

What is the inference we must draw herefrom? Why, that both repentance, rightly understood, and the practice of all good works —works of piety, as well as works of mercy (now properly so called, since they spring from faith), are, in some sense, necessary to sanctification.

I say, 'repentance rightly understood'; for this must not be confounded with the former repentance. The repentance consequent upon justification is widely different from that which is antecedent to it. This implies no guilt, no sense of condemnation, no consciousness of the wrath of God. It does not suppose any doubt of the favour of God, or any 'fear that hath torment.' It is properly a conviction, wrought by the Holy Ghost, of the *sin* which still *remains* in our heart; of the θρονημα σ αρκος the: carnal mind, which 'does still *remain*' (as our Church speaks) 'even in them that are regenerate'; although it does no long *reign*; it has not now dominion over them. It is a conviction of our proneness to evil, of an heart bent to backsliding, of the still continuing tendency of the flesh to lust against the spirit. Sometimes, unless we continually watch and pray, it lusteth to pride, sometimes to anger, sometimes to love of the world, love of ease, love of honour, or love of pleasure more than of God. It is a conviction of the tendency of our heart to self-will, to atheism, or idolatry; and above all, to unbelief; whereby, in a thousand ways, and under a thousand pretenses, we are ever departing, more or less, from the living God.

With this conviction of the sin remaining in our hearts, there is joined a clear conviction of the sin remaining in our lives; still *cleaving* to all our words and actions. In the best of these we now discern a mixture of evil, either in the spirit, the matter, or the manner of them; something that could not endure the righteous judgement of God, were He extreme to mark what is done amiss. Where we least suspected it, we find a taint of pride or self-will, of unbelief or idolatry; so that we are now more ashamed of our best duties than formerly of our worst sins; and hence we cannot but feel that these are so far from having anything meritorious in them, yea, so far from being able to stand in sight of the divine justice, that for those also we should be guilty before God, were it not for the blood of the covenant.

Experience shows that, together with this conviction of sin *remaining* in our hearts, and *cleaving* to all our words and actions; as well as the guilt which on account thereof we should incur, were we not continually sprinkled with the atoning blood; one thing more is impled in this repentance; namely, a conviction of our helplessness, of our utter inability to think one good thought, or to form one good desire; and much more to speak one word aright, or to perform one good action, but through His free, almighty grace, first preventing us, and then accompanying us every moment.

'But what good works are those, the practice of which you affirm to be necessary to sanctification?' First, all works of piety; such as public prayer, family prayer, and praying in our closet; receiving the supper of the Lord; searching the Scriptures, by hearing, reading, meditation; and using such a measure of fasting or abstinence as our bodily health allows.

Secondly, all works of mercy; whether they relate to the bodies or souls of men; such as feeding the hungry, clothing the naked, entertaining the stranger, visiting those that are in prison, or sick, or variously afflicted; such as the endeavouring to instruct the ignorant, to awaken the stupid sinner, to quicken the lukewarm, to confirm the wavering, to comfort the feeble-minded, to succour the tempted, or contribute in any manner to the saving of souls from death. This is the repentance, and these the 'fruits meet for repentance,' which are necessary to full sanctification. This is the way wherein God hath appointed His children to wait for complete salvation.

Hence may appear the extreme mischievousness of that seemingly innocent opinion, that there is no sin in a believer; that all sin is destroyed, root and branch, the moment a man is justified. By totally preventing that repentance, it quite blocks up the way to sanctification. There is no place for repentance in him who believes there is no sin either in his life or heart; consequently, there is no place for his being perfected in love, to which that repentance is indispensably necessary.

Hence, it may likewise appear, that there is no possible danger in *thus* expecting full salvation. For suppose we were mistaken, suppose no such blessing ever was or can be attained, yet we lose nothing; nay, that very expectation quickens us in using all the talents which God has given us; yea, in improving them all, so that when our Lord cometh, He will receive His own with increase.

But to return. Though it be allowed, that both this repentance and its fruits are necessary to full salvation; yet they are not necessary either in the same sense with faith, or in the same degree.—Not in the *same degree*; for these fruits are only necessary *conditionally*, if there be time and opportunity for them; otherwise a man may be sanctified without them. But he cannot be sanctified without faith. Likewise, let a man have ever so much of this repentance, or ever so many good works, yet all this does not at all avail; he is not sanctified till he believes. But the moment he believes, with or without those fruits, yea, with more or less of this repentance, he is sanctified.—Not in the *same sense*; for this repentance and these fruits are only *remotely* necessary—necessary in order to the continuance of his faith, as well as the increase of it; whereas faith is *immediately* and *directly* necessary to sanctification. It remains, that faith is the only condition which is *immediately* and *proximately* necessary to sanctification.

'But what is that faith whereby we are sanctified,—saved from sin, and perfected in love?' It is a divine evidence and conviction, first, that God hath promised it in the holy Scripture. Till we are thoroughly satisfied of this, there is no moving one step further. And one would imagine there needed not one word more to satisfy a reasonable man of this, than the ancient promise, 'Then will I circumcise thy heart, and the heart of thy seed, to love the Lord thy God with all thy heart, and with all thy soul, and with all thy mind.' How clearly does this express the being perfected in love!—how strongly imply the being saved from all sin! For as long as love takes up the whole heart, what room is there for sin therein?

It is a divine evidence and conviction, secondly, that what God hath promised He is able to perform. Admitting, therefore, that 'with men it is impossible; to 'bring a clean thing out of an unclean,' to purify the heart from all sin, and to fill it with all holiness; yet this creates no difficulty in the case, seeing 'with God all things are possible.' And surely no one ever imagined it was possible to any power less than that of the Almighty! But if God speaks, it shall be done. God saith, 'Let there be light; and there' is 'light'!

It is, thirdly, a divine evidence and conviction that He is able and willing to do it now. And why not? Is not a moment to Him the same as a thousand years? He cannot want more time to accomplish whatever is His will. And He cannot want to stay for any more *worthiness* or *fitness* in the persons He is pleased to honour. We may therefore boldly say, at any point of time, 'Now is the day of salvation!' 'Today, if ye will hear His voice, harden not your hearts!' 'Behold, all things are now ready; come unto the marriage!'

To this confidence, that God is both able and willing to sanctify us now, there needs to be added one thing more,—a divine evidence and conviction that He doeth it. In that hour it is done: God says to the inmost soul, 'According to thy faith be it unto thee!' Then the soul is pure from every spot of sin; it is clean 'from all unrighteousness.' The believer then experiences the deep meaning of those solemn words, 'If we walk in the light as He is in the light, we have fellowship one with another, and the blood of Jesus Christ His Son cleanseth us from all sin.'

'But does God work this great work in the soul gradually or instantaneously?' Perhaps it may be gradually wrought in some; I mean in this sense—they do not advert to the particular moment wherein sin ceases to be. But it is infinitely desirable, were it the will of God, that it should be done instantaneously; that the Lord should destroy sin 'by the breath of His mouth,' in a moment, in the twinkling of an eye. And so He generally does; a plain fact, of which there is evidence enough to satisfy any unprejudiced person. *Thou* therefore look for it every moment! Look for it in the way above described; in all those *good works* whereunto thou art 'created anew in Christ Jesus.' There is then no danger; you can be no worse, if you are no better, for that expectation. For were you to be disappointed of your hope, still you lose nothing. But you shall not be disappointed of your hope; it will come, and will not tarry. Look for it then every day, every hour, every moment! Why not this hour, this moment? Certainly you may look for it *now*, if you believe it is by faith. And by this token you may surely know whether you seek it by faith or by works. If by works, you want something to be done *first*, *before* you are sanctified. You think, I must first *be* or *do* thus or thus. Then you are seeking it by works unto this day. If you seek it by faith, you may expect it *as* you are; and if as you are, then expect it *now*. It is of importance to observe, that there is an inseparable connexion between these three points,—expect it *by faith*; expect it as you *are*; and expect it *now*. To deny one of them, is to deny them all; to allow one, is to allow them all. Do *you* believe we are sanctified by faith? Be true then to your principle; and look for this blessing just as you are, neither better nor worse; as a poor sinner that has still nothing to pay, nothing to plead, but 'Christ *died*.' And if you look for it as you are, then expect it *now*. Stay for nothing; why should you? Christ is ready; and He is all you want. He is waiting for you; He is at the door! Let your inmost soul cry out,

> *Come in, come in, Thou heavenly Guest!*
> *Nor hence again remove;*
> *But sup with me, and let the feast*
> *Be everlasting love.*

2
The Circumcision of the Heart

Circumcision is that of the heart, in the spirit, and not in the letter. - Rom. 2:29

It is the melancholy remark of an excellent man, that he who now preaches the most essential duties of Christianity runs the hazard of being esteemed, by a great part of his hearers, 'a setter forth of new doctrines.' Most men have so *lived away* the substance of that religion, the profession whereof they still retain, that no sooner are any of those truths proposed which difference the Spirit of Christ from the spirit of the world, than they cry out, 'Thou bringest strange things to our ears; we would know what these things mean': though he is only preaching to them 'Jesus and the resurrection,' with the necessary consequence of it.—If Christ be risen, ye ought then to die unto the world, and to live wholly unto God.

A hard saying this to the natural man, who is alive unto the world, and dead unto God; and one that he will not readily be persuaded to receive as the truth of God, unless it be so qualified in the interpretation, as to have neither use or significancy left. He 'receiveth not the' words 'of the Spirit of God, 'taken in their plain and obvious meaning; 'they are foolishness unto him, neither' indeed 'can he know them, because they are spiritually discerned'; they are perceivable only by that spiritual sense, which in him was never yet awakened; for want of which he must reject, as idle fancies of men, what are both the wisdom and the power of God.

That 'circumcision is that of the heart, in the spirit, and not in the letter'—that the distinguishing mark of a true follower of Christ, of one who is in a state of acceptance with God, is not either outward circumcision, or baptism, or any other outward form, but a right state of soul, a mind and spirit renewed after the image of Him that created it—is one of those important truths that can only be spiritually discerned. And this the Apostle himself intimates in the next words: 'Whose praise is not of men, but of God.' As if he had said, 'Expect not, whoever thou art, who thus followest thy great Master, that the world, the men who follow Him not, will say, "Well done, good and faithful servant!" Know that the circumcision of the heart, the seal of thy calling, is foolishness with the world. Be content to wait for thy applause till the day of thy Lord's appearing. In that day shalt thou have praise of God, in the great assembly of men and angels.'

I design, first, particularly to inquire, wherein this circumcision of the heart consists; and, secondly, to mention some reflections that naturally arise from such an inquiry.

I. I am, first, to inquire, wherein that circumcision of the heart consists, which will receive the praise of God. In general we may observe, it is that habitual disposition of soul which, in the sacred writings, is termed holiness; and which directly implies, the being cleansed from sin, 'from all filthiness both of flesh and spirit'; and, by consequence, the being endured with those virtues which were also in Christ Jesus; the being so 'renewed in the spirit of our mind,' as to be 'perfect as our Father in heaven is perfect.'

To be more particular: circumcision of heart implies humility, faith, hope, and charity. Humility, a right judgment of ourselves, cleanses our minds from those high conceits of our own perfections, from that undue opinion of our own abilities and attainments, which are the genuine fruit of a corrupted nature. This entirely cuts off that vain thought, 'I am rich, and wise, and have need of nothing'; and convinces us that we are by nature 'wretched, and poor, and miserable, and blind, and naked.' It convinces us, that in our best estate we are, of ourselves, all sin and vanity; that confusion, and ignorance, and error reign over our understanding; that unreasonable, earthly, sensual, devilish passions usurp authority over our will; in a word, that there is no whole part in our soul, that all the foundations of our nature are out of course.

At the same time we are convinced, that we are not sufficient of ourselves to help ourselves; that, without the Spirit of God, we can do nothing but add sin to sin; that it is He alone who worketh in us by His almighty power, either to will or do that which is good; it being as impossible for us even to think a good thought, without the supernatural assistance of His Spirit, as to create ourselves, or to renew our whole souls in righteousness and true holiness.

A sure effect of our having formed this right judgment of the sinfulness and helplessness of our nature, is a disregard of that 'honor which cometh of man,' which is usually paid to some supposed excellency in us. He who knows himself, neither desires nor values the applause which he knows he deserves not. It is therefore 'a very small thing with him, to be judged by man's judgement.' He has all reason to think, by comparing what it has said, either for or against him, with what he feels in his own breast, that the world, as well as the god of this world, was 'a liar from the beginning.' And even as to those who are not of the world; thought he would choose, if it were the will of God, that they should account of him as of one desirous to be found a faithful steward of his Lord's goods, if haply this might be a means of enabling him to be of more use to his fellow servants, yet as this is the one end of his wishing for their approbation, so he does not at all rest upon it; for he is assured, that whatever God wills, he can never want instruments to perform; since He is able, even of these stones, to raise up servants to do His pleasure.

This is that lowliness of mind, which they have learned of Christ, who follow His example and tread in His steps. And this knowledge of their disease, whereby they are more and more cleansed from one part of it, pride and vanity, disposes them to embrace, with a willing mind, the second thing implied in circumcision of the heart,—that faith which alone is able to make them whole, which is the one medicine given under heaven to heal their sickness.

The best guide of the blind, the surest light of them that are in darkness, the most perfect instructor of the foolish, is faith. But it must be such a faith as is 'mighty through God, to the pulling down of strongholds'—to the overturning all the prejudices of corrupt reason, all the false maxims revered among men, all evil customs and habits, all that 'wisdom of the world which is foolishness with God'; as 'casteth down imaginations,' reasonings, 'and every high thing that exalteth itself against the knowledge of God, and bringeth into captivity every thought to the obedience of Christ.'

'All things are possible to him that thus believeth.' 'The eyes of his understanding being enlightened,' he sees what is his calling; even to glorify God, who hath bought him with so high a price, in his body and in his spirit, which now are God's by redemption, as well as by creation. He feels what is 'the exceeding greatness of His power,' who, as He raised up Christ from the dead, so is able to quicken us, dead in sin, 'by His Spirit which dwelleth in us.' ' This is the victory which overcometh the world, even our faith'; that faith, which is not only an unshaken assent to all that God hath revealed in Scripture—and in particular to those important truths. 'Jesus Christ came into the world to save sinners,' 'He bare our sins in His own body on the tree,' 'He is the propitiation for our sins, and not for ours only, but also for the sins of the whole world,'—but likewise the revelation of Christ in our hearts; a divine evidence or conviction of His love. His free, unmerited love to me a sinner; a sure confidence in His pardoning mercy, wrought in us by the Holy Ghost; a confidence, whereby every true believer is enabled to bear witness, 'I know that my Redeemer liveth,' that I have an 'Advocate with Father,' and that 'Jesus Christ the righteous' is my Lord, and 'the propitiation for my sins'—I know He hath 'loved me, and given Himself for me'—He hath reconciled me, even me, to God; and I 'have redemption through His blood, even the forgiveness of sins.'

Such a faith as this cannot fail to show evidently the power of Him that inspires it, by delivering His children from the yoke of sin, and 'purging their consciences from dead works'; by strengthening them so, that they are no longer constrained to obey sin in the desires thereof; but instead of 'yielding their members unto it, as instruments of unrighteousness,' they now 'yield themselves' entirely 'unto God, as those that are alive from the dead.'

Those who are thus by faith born of God have also strong consolation through hope. This is the next thing which the circumcision of the heart implies; even the testimony of their own spirit with the Spirit which witnesses in their hearts that they are the children of God. Indeed it is the same Spirit who works in them that clear and cheerful confidence that their heart is upright toward God; that good assurance, that they now do, through His grace, the things which are acceptable in His sight; that they are now in the path which leadeth to life, and shall, by the mercy of God, endure therein to the end. It is He who giveth them a lively expectation of receiving all good things at God's hand; a joyous prospect of that crown of glory which is reserved in heaven for them. By this anchor a Christian is kept steady in the midst of the waves of this troublesome world, and preserved from striking upon either of those fatal rocks,—presumption or despair. He is neither discouraged by the misconceived severity of his Lord, nor does he 'despise the riches of His goodness.' He neither apprehends the difficulties of the race set before him to be greater than he has strength to conquer, nor expects them to be so little as to yield in the conquest till he has put forth all his strength. The experience he already has in the Christian warfare, as it assured him his 'labour is not in vain,' if whatever his hand findeth to do, he doeth it with his might'; so it forbids his entertaining so vain a thought, as that he can otherwise gain any advantage; as that any virtue can be shown, any praise attained, by faint hearts and feeble hands; or, indeed, by any but those who pursue the same course with the great

Apostle of the Gentiles; 'I,' says he, 'so run, not as uncertainly; so fight I, not as one that beateth the air; but I keep under my body, and bring it unto subjection, lest, by any means, when I have preached to others, I myself should be castaway.'

By the same discipline is every good soldier of Christ to inure himself to endure hardship. Confirmed and strengthened by this, he will be able not only to renounce the works of darkness, but every appetite too, and every affection, which is not subject to the law of God. For 'every one,' saith St. John, 'who hath this hope, purifieth himself even as He is pure.' It is his daily care, by the grace of God in Christ, and through the blood of the covenant, to purge the inmost recesses of his soul from the lusts that before possessed and defiled it; from uncleanness, and envy, and malice, and wrath; from every passion and temper that is after the flesh, that either springs from or cherishes his native corruption; as well knowing, that he whose very body is the temple of God, ought to admit into it nothing common or unclean; and that holiness becometh that house for ever, where the Spirit of holiness vouchsafes to dwell.

Yet lackest thou one thing, whosoever thou art, that to a deep humility, and a steadfast faith, hast joined a lively hope, and thereby in a good measure cleansed thy heart from its inbred pollution. If thou wilt be perfect, add to all these, charity; add love, and thou hast the circumcision of the heart. 'Love is the fulfilling of the law, the end of the commandment.' Very excellent things are spoken of love; it is the essence, the spirit, the life of all virtue. It is not only the first and great command, but it is all the commandments in one. 'Whatsoever things are just, whatsoever things are pure, whatsoever things are amiable,' or honorable; 'if there be any virtue, if there be any praise,' they are all comprised in this one word, —love. In this is perfection, and glory, and happiness. The royal law of heaven and earth is this. 'Thou shalt love the Lord thy God with all thy heart, and with all thy soul, and with all thy mind, and with all thy strength.'

Not that this forbids us to love anything besides God; it implies that we love our brother also. Nor yet does it forbid us (as some have strangely imagined) to take pleasure in anything but God. To suppose this, is to suppose the Fountain of holiness is directly the author of sin; since He has inseparably annexed pleasure to the use of those creatures which are necessary to sustain the life He has given us. This, therefore, can never be the meaning of His command. What the real sense of it is, both our blessed Lord and His Apostles tell us too frequently, and too plainly, to be misunderstood. They all with one mouth bear witness, that the true meaning of those several declarations, 'The Lord thy God is one Lord'; 'Thou shalt have no other gods but Me'; 'Thou shalt love the Lord thy God with all thy strength'; 'Thou shalt cleave unto Him'; 'The desire of thy soul shall

be to His name,' is no other than this: The one
perfect God shall be your one ultimate end. One
thing shall ye desire for its own sake,—the frui-
tion of Him that is All in all. One happiness
shall ye propose to your souls, even as union
with Him that made them; the having 'fellowship with the Father and the Son'; the being
joined to the Lord in one Spirit. One design you
are to pursue to the end of time,—the enjoy-
ment of God in time and in eternity. Desire other
things, so far as they tend to this. Love the creature, as it leads to the Creator. But in every step
you take, be this the glorious point that termi-
nates your view. Let every affection, and
thought, and word, and work, be subordinate to
this. Whatever ye desire or fear, whatever ye
seek or shun, whatever ye think, speak or do,
be it in order to your happiness in God, the sole
End, as well as Source, of your being.

Have no end, no ultimate end, but God. Thus
our Lord: 'One thing is needful'; and if thine
eye be singly fixed on this one thing, 'thy whole
body shall be full of light.' Thus St. Paul: 'This
one thing I do: I press toward the mark, for the
prize of the high calling in Christ Jesus.' Thus
St. James: 'Cleanse your hands, ye sinners; and
purify your hearts, ye double-minded.' Thus St.
John: 'Love not the world, neither the things
that are in the world. For all that is in the world,
the lust of the flesh, the lust of the eye, and the
pride of life, is not of the Father, but is of the
world.' The seeking happiness in what grati-
fies either the desire of the flesh, by agreeably

striking upon the outward senses; the desire of the eye, of the imagination, by its novelty, greatness, or beauty; or the pride of life, whether by pomp, grandeur, power, or, the usual consequence of them, applause and admiration,—'is not of the Father,' cometh not from, neither is approved by, the Father of spirits: 'but of the world'; it is the distinguishing mark of those who will not have Him to reign over them.

II. Thus have I particularly inquired, what that circumcision of heart is, which will obtain the praise of God. I am, in the second place, to mention some reflections that naturally arise from such an inquiry, as a plain rule whereby every man may judge of himself, whether he be of the world or of God.

And, first, it is clear from what has been said, that no man has a title to the praise of God, unless his heart is circumcised by humility; unless he is little, and base, and vile in his own eyes; unless he is deeply convinced of that inbred 'corruption of his nature,' 'whereby he is very far gone from original righteousness,' being prone to all evil, averse to all good, corrupt and abominable; having a 'carnal mind which is enmity against God, and is not subject to the law of God, nor indeed can be'; unless he continually feels in his inmost soul, that without the Spirit of God resting upon him, he can neither think, nor desire, nor speak, nor act anything good, or well-pleasing in His sight.

No man, I say, has a title to the praise of God, till he feels his want of God; not indeed, till he

seeketh that 'honour which cometh of God'
only; and neither desires nor pursues that which
cometh of man, unless so far only as it tends to
this.

Another truth, which naturally follows from
what has been said, is, that none shall obtain
the honour that cometh of God, unless his heart
be circumcised by faith; even a 'faith of the
operation of God'; unless, refusing to be any
longer led by his senses, appetites, or passions,
or even by that blind leader of the blind, so idol-
ized by the world, natural reason, he lives and
walks by faith; directs every step, as 'seeing
Him that is invisible'; 'looks not at the things
that are seen, which are temporal, but at the
things that are not seen, which are eternal'; and
governs all his desires, designs, and thoughts,
all his actions and conversations, as one who is
entered in within the veil, where Jesus sits at
the right hand of God.

It were to be wished, that they were better
acquainted with this faith who employ much of
their time and pains in laying another foundation; in grounding religion on the eternal *fitness* of things, on the intrinsic *excellence* of virtue, and the *beauty* of actions flowing from it;
on the *reasons*, as they term them, of good and
evil, and the *relations*, of beings to each other.
Either these accounts of the grounds of Christian duty coincide with the scriptural, or not. If
they do, why are well-meaning men perplexed,
and drawn from the weightier matters of the law,
by a cloud of terms, whereby the easiest truths

are explained into obscurity? If they are not, then it behoves them to consider who is the author of this new doctrine; whether he is likely to be an angel from heaven, who preacheth another gospel than that of Christ Jesus; though, if he were, God, not we, hath pronounced his sentence: 'Let him be accursed.'

Our gospel, as it knows no other foundation of good works than faith, or of faith than Christ, so it clearly informs us, we are not His disciples while we either deny Him to be the Author, or His Spirit to be the Inspirer and Perfecter, both of our faith and works. 'If any man have not the Spirit of Christ, he is none of his.' He alone can quicken those who are dead unto God, can breathe into them the breath of Christian life, and so prevent, accompany, and follow them with His grace, as to bring their good desires to good effect. And, 'as many as are thus led by the Spirit of God, they are the sons of God.' This is God's short and plain account of true religion and virtue; and 'other foundation can no man lay.'

From what has been said, we may, thirdly, learn, that none is truly 'led by the Spirit,' unless that 'Spirit bear witness with his spirit, that he is a child of God'; unless he see the prize and the crown before him, and 'rejoice in hope of the glory of God.' So greatly have they erred who have taught that in serving God, we ought not to have a view to our own happiness! Nay, but we often and expressly taught of God, to have 'respect unto the recompense of reward'; to balance the toil with the 'joy set before us,' these 'light afflictions' with that 'exceeding weight of glory.' Yea, we are 'aliens to the covenant of promise,' we are 'without God in the world,' until God, 'of His abundant mercy, hath begotten us again unto a living hope of the inheritance incorruptible, undefiled, and that fadeth not away.'

But if these things are so, it is high time for those persons to deal faithfully with their own souls, who are so far from finding in themselves this joyful assurance that they fulfill the terms, and shall obtain the promises, of that covenant, as to quarrel with the covenant itself, and blaspheme the terms of it; to complain, they are too severe; and that no man ever did or shall live up to them. What is this but to reproach God, as if He were an hard Master, requiring of His servants more than He enables them to perform? —as if He had mocked the helpless works of His hands, by binding them to impossibilities; by commanding them to overcome, where neither their own strength nor His grace was sufficient for them?

These blasphemers might almost persuade those to imagine themselves guiltless, who, in the contrary extreme, hope to fulfill the commands of God without taking any pains at all. Vain hope! that a child of Adam should ever expect to see the kingdom of Christ and of God without striving, without *agonizing*, first 'to enter in at the strait gate'; that one who was 'conceived and born in sin,' and whose 'inward parts are very wickedness,' should once entertain a thought of being 'purified as his Lord is pure,' unless he tread in His steps, and 'take up his cross daily,' unless he 'cut off his right hand,' and 'pluck out the right eye, and cast it from him'; that he should ever dream of shaking off his old opinions, passions, tempers, of being 'sanctified throughout in spirit, soul, and body,' without a constant and continued course of general self-denial!

What less than this can we possibly infer from the above-cited words of St. Paul, who, living 'in infirmities, in reproaches, in necessities, in persecutions, in distresses' for Christ's sake; who, being full of 'signs and wonders, and mighty deeds,' who, having been 'caught up into the third heaven,'—yet reckoned, as a late author strongly expresses it, that all his virtues would be insecure, and even his salvation in danger, without this constant self-denial? So run I,' says he, 'not as uncertainly; so fight I, not as one that beateth the air': by which he plainly teaches us, that he who does not thus run, who does not thus deny himself daily, does run uncertainly, and fighteth to as little purpose as he that 'beateth the air.'

To as little purpose does he talk of 'fighting the fight of faith,' as vainly hope to attain the crown of incorruption (as we may, lastly, infer from the preceding observations), whose heart is not circumcised by love. Love, cutting off both the lust of the flesh, the lust of the eye, and the pride of life—engaging the whole man, body, soul, and spirit, in the ardent pursuit of that one object—is so essential to a child of God, that without it, whosoever liveth is counteth dead before Him. 'Thought I speak with the tongues of men and of angels, and have not love, I am as sounding brass, or a tinkling cymbal. Though I have the gift of prophecy, and understand all mysteries, and all knowledge; and though I have all faith, so as to remove mountains, and have not love, I am nothing.' Nay, 'though I give all my goods to feed the poor, and my body to be burned, and have not love, it profiteth me nothing.'

Here, then, is the sum of the perfect law: this is the true circumcision of the heart. Let the spirit return to God that gave it, with the whole train of its affections. 'Unto the place from whence all the rivers came,' thither let them flow again. Other sacrifices from us He would not; but the living sacrifice of the heart He hath chosen. Let it be continually offered up to God through Christ, in flames of holy love. And let no creature be suffered to share with Him: for He is a jealous God. His throne will He not divide with another: He will reign without a rival. Be no design, no desire admitted there, but what has Him for its ultimate object. This is the way wherein those children of God once walked, who, being dead, still speak to us: 'Desire not to live but to praise His name: let all your thoughts, words, and works tend to His glory. Set your heart firm on Him, and on other things only as they are in and from Him. Let your soul be filled with so entire a love of Him that you may love nothing but for His sake.' 'Have a pure intention of heart, a steadfast regard to His glory in all your actions.' 'Fix your eye upon the blessed hope of your calling, and make all the things of the world minister unto it.' For then, and not till then, is that 'mind in us which was also in Christ Jesus'; when, in every motion of our heart, in every word of our tongue, in every work of our hands, we 'pursue nothing but in relation to Him, and in subordination to His pleasure'; when we, too, neither think, nor speak, nor act, to fulfill our 'own will, but the will of Him that sent us'; when, whether we 'eat or drink, or whatever we do, we do all to the glory of God.'

3
The Repentance of Believers

It is generally supposed, that repentance and
faith are only the gate of religion; that they are
necessary only at the beginning of our Christian course, when we are setting out in the way
to the kingdom. And this may seem to be confirmed by the great Apostle, where, exhorting
the Hebrew Christians to 'go on to perfection,'
he teaches them to *leave* these first 'principles
of the doctrine of Christ'; 'not laying again the
foundation of repentance from dead works, and
of faith towards God'; which must at least mean,
that they should comparatively leave these, that
at first took up all their thoughts, in order to
'press forward toward the prize of the high calling of God in Christ Jesus.'

And this is undoubtedly true, that there is a
repentance and a faith, which are, more especially, necessary at the beginning: a repentance,
which is a conviction of our utter sinfulness,
and guiltiness, and helplessness; and which pre-
cedes our receiving that kingdom of God,
which, our Lord observes, is 'within us'; and a
faith, whereby we receive that kingdom, even
'righteousness, and peace, and joy in the Holy
Ghost.'

But, notwithstanding this, there is also a repentance and a faith (taking the words in another sense, a sense not quite the same, nor yet

entirely different) which are requisite after we have 'believed the gospel'; yea, and in every subsequent stage of our Christian course, or we cannot 'run the race which is set before us.' And this repentance and faith are as full as necessary, in order to our *continuance* and *growth* in grace, as the former faith and repentance were, in order to our entering into the kingdom of God.

But in what sense are we to repent and believe, after we are justified? This is an important question, and worthy of being considered with the utmost attention.

And, first, in what sense are we to repent?

Repentance frequently means an inward change, a change of mind from sin to holiness. But we now speak of it in a quite different sense, as it is one kind of self-knowledge, and knowing ourselves sinners, yea, guilty, helpless sinners, even though we know we are children of God.

Indeed when we first know this; when we first find redemption in the blood of Jesus; when the love of God is first shed abroad in our hearts, and His kingdom set up therein; it is natural to suppose that we are no longer sinners, that all our sins are not only covered but destroyed.

As we do not then feel any evil in our hearts, we readily imagine none is there. Nay, some well-meaning men have imagined this not only at that time, but ever after; having persuaded themselves, that when they were justified, they were entirely sanctified: yea, they have laid it down as a general rule, in spite of Scripture, reason, and experience. These sincerely believe, and earnestly maintain, that all sin is destroyed when we are justified; and that there is no sin in the heart of a believer; but that it is altogether clean from that moment. But though we readily acknowledge, 'he that believeth is born of God,' and 'he that is born of God doth not commit sin'; yet we cannot allow that he does not *feel* it within: it does not *reign, but it does remain*. And a conviction of the sin which *remains* in our heart, is one great branch of the repentance we are now speaking of.

For it is seldom long before he who imagined all sin was gone, feels there is still *pride* in his heart. He is convinced both that in many respects he has thought of himself more highly than he ought to think, and that he has taken to himself the praise of something he had received, and gloried in it as though he had not received it; and yet he knows he is in the favour of God. He cannot, and ought not to, 'cast away his confidence.' 'The Spirit' still 'witnesses with' his 'spirit, that he is a child of God.'

Nor is it long before he feels *self-will* in his heart; even a will contrary to the will of God. A will every man must inevitably have, as long as he has an understanding. This is an essential part of human nature, indeed of the nature of every intelligent being. Our blessed Lord Himself had a will as a man; otherwise He had not been a man. But His human will was invariably subject to the will of His Father. At all times, and on all occasions, even in the deepest affliction, He could say, 'Not as I will, but as Thou wilt.' But this is not the case at all times, even with a true believer in Christ. He frequently finds his will more or less exalting itself against the will of God. He wills something, because it is pleasing to nature, which is not pleasing to God; and he nills (is averse from) something, because it is painful to nature, which is the will of God concerning him. Indeed, suppose he continues in the faith, he fights against it with all his might: but his very thing implies that it really exists, and that he is conscious of it.

Now self-will, as well as pride, is a species of *idolatry*; and both are directly contrary to the love of God. The same observation may be made concerning the *love of the world*. But this likewise even true believers are liable to feel in themselves; and every one of them does feel it, more or less, sooner or later, in one branch or another. It is true, when he first 'passes from death unto life,' he desires nothing more but God. He can truly say, 'All my desire is unto Thee, and unto the remembrance of Thy name': 'Whom have I in heaven but Thee? and there is none upon earth that I desire beside Thee.' But it is not so always. In process of time he will feel again, though perhaps only for a few moments, either 'the desire of the flesh,' or 'the desire of the eye,' or 'the pride of life. Nay, if he does not continually watch and pray, he may find *lust* reviving; yea, and thrusting sore at him that he may fall, till he has scarce any strength left in him. He may feel the assaults of *inordi-*

nate affection; yea, a strong propensity to '<u>love the creature more than the Creator</u>'; whether it be a child, a parent, a husband, or wife, or 'the friend that is as his own soul.' He may feel, in a thousand various ways, a desire of earthly things or pleasures. In the same proportion he will forget God, not seeking his happiness in Him, and consequently being a 'lover of pleasure more than a lover of God.'

If he does not keep himself every moment, he will again feel the *desire of the eye*; the desire of gratifying his imagination with something great, or beautiful, or uncommon. In how many ways does this desire assault the soul! Perhaps with regard to the poorest trifles, such as dress, or furniture; things never designed to satisfy the appetite of an immortal spirit. Yet, how natural is it for us, even after we have 'tasted of the powers of the world to come,' to sink again into these foolish, low desires of things that perish in the using! How hard is it, even for those who know in whom they have believed, to conquer but one branch of the desire of the eye, *curiosity*; constantly to trample it under their feet; to desire nothing merely because it is new!

And how hard is it even for the children of God wholly to conquer the *pride of life*! St. John seems to mean by this nearly the same with <u>what the world terms 'the sense of honour.'</u> This is no other than a desire of, and delight in, 'the honour that cometh of men'; a desire and love <u>of praise</u>; and, which is always joined with it, a proportionable *fear of dispraise*. Nearly allied to this is *evil shame*; the being ashamed of that wherein we ought to glory. And this is seldom divided from the *fear of man*, which brings a thousand snares upon the soul. Now where is he, even among those that seem strong in the faith, who does not find in himself a degree of all these evil tempers? So that even these are but in part 'crucified to the world'; for the evil root still remains in their heart.

And do we not feel other tempers, which are as contrary to the love of our neighbour as these are to the love of God? The love of our neighbour 'thinketh no evil.' Do not we find anything of the kind? Do we never find any *jealousies*, any evil *surmisings*, any groundless or unreasonable suspicions? He that is clear in these respects, let him cast the first stone at his neighbour. Who does not sometimes feel other tempers or inward motions, which he knows are contrary to brotherly love? If nothing of *malice*, *hatred*, or *bitterness*, is there no touch of *envy*; particularly toward those who enjoy some real or supposed good, which we desire, but cannot attain? Do we never find any degree of *resentment*, when we are injured or affronted; especially by those whom we peculiarly loved, and whom we had most laboured to help or oblige? Does injustice or ingratitude never excite in us any desire of *revenge*? any desire of returning evil for evil, instead of 'overcoming evil with good'? This also shows, how much is still in our heart, which is contrary to the love of our neighbour.

Covetousness, in every kind and degree, is certainly as contrary to this as to the love of God; whether φιλαργυρια, the love of money, which is too frequently 'the root of all evil'; πλεονεξια literally, a desire of *having more*, or increasing in substance. And how few, even of the real children of God, are entirely free from both! Indeed one great man, Martin Luther, used to say, he 'never had any covetousness in him' (not only in his converted state, but) 'ever since he was born.' But, if so, I would scruple to say, he was the only man born of a woman (except Him that was God as well as man), who had not, who was born without it. Nay, I believe never was any one born of God, that lived any considerable time after, who did not feel more or less of it many times, especially in the latter sense. We may therefore set it down as an undoubted truth, that covetousness, together with pride, and self-will, and anger, remain in the hearts even of them that are justified.

It is their experiencing this, which has inclined so many serious persons to understand the latter part of the seventh chapter to the Romans, not of them that are 'under the law,' that are convinced of sin, which is undoubtedly the meaning of the Apostle, but of them that are 'under grace'; that are 'justified freely through the redemption that is in Christ.' And it is most certain, they are thus far right,—there does still *remain*, even in them that are justified, a *mind* which is in some measure *carnal* (so the Apostle tells even the believers at Corinth, 'Ye are carnal'); an *heart bent to backsliding*, still ever ready to 'depart from the living God'; a propensity to pride, self-will, anger, revenge, love of the world, yea, and all evil: a root of bitterness, which, if the restraint were taken off for a moment, would instantly spring up; yea, such a depth of corruption, as, without clear light from God, we cannot possibly conceive. And a conviction of all this sin *remaining* in *their hearts* is the repentance which belongs to them that are justified.

But we should likewise be convinced, that as sin remains in our hearts, so it cleaves to all our words and actions. Indeed it is to be feared, that many of our words are more than mixed with sin; that they are sinful altogether; for such undoubtedly is all *uncharitable conversation*; all which does not spring from brotherly love; all which does not agree with that golden rule, 'What ye would that others should do to you, even so do unto them.' Of this kind is all backbiting, all tale-bearing, all whispering, all evil-speaking, that is, repeating the faults of absent persons; for none would have others repeat his faults when he is absent. Now how few are there, even among believers, who are in no degree guilty of this; who steadily observe the good old rule, 'Of the dead and the absent, nothing but good!' And suppose they do, do they likewise abstain from *unprofitable conversation*? Yet all this is unquestionably sinful, and 'grieves the Holy Spirit of God'; yea, and for every idle word that men shall speak, they shall give an account in the day of judgement.'

But let it be supposed, that they continually 'watch and pray,' and so do 'not enter into' this 'temptation'; that they constantly set a watch before their mouth, and keep the door of their lips; suppose they exercise themselves herein, that *all* their 'conversation may be in grace, seasoned with salt, and meet to minister grace to the hearers': yet do they not daily slide into useless discourse, notwithstanding all their caution? And even when they endeavour to speak for God, are their words pure, free from unholy mixtures? Do they find nothing wrong in their very *intention*? Do they speak merely to please God, and not partly to please themselves? Is it wholly to do the will of God, and not their own will also? Or, if they being with a single eye, do they go on 'looking unto Jesus,' and talking with Him all the time they are talking with their neighbour? When they are reproving sin, do they feel no anger or unkind temper to the sinner? When they are instructing the ignorant, do they not find any pride, any self-preference? When they are comforting the afflicted, or provoking one another to love and to good works, do they never perceive any inward self-commendation: *'Now you have spoke well'*? Or any vanity—a desire that others should think so, and esteem them on the account? In some or all of these respects, how much sin cleaves to the best *conversation* even of believers! The conviction of which is another branch of the repentance which belongs to them that are justified.

And how much sin, if their conscience is thoroughly awake, may they find cleaving to *their actions* also! Nay, are there not many of these, which, though they are such as the world would not condemn, yet cannot be commended, no, nor excused, if we judge by the Word of God? Are there not many of their actions which, they themselves know, are not to the glory of God? many, wherein they did not even aim at this; which were not undertaken with an eye to God? And of those that were, are there not many, wherein their eye is not singly fixed on God—wherein they are doing their own will, at least as much as His; and seeking to please themselves as much, if not more, than to please God? And while they are endeavouring to do good to their neighbor, do they not feel wrong tempers of various kinds? Hence their good actions, so called, are far from being strictly such; being polluted with such a mixture of evil: such are their works of *mercy*. And is there not the same mixture in their works of *piety*? While they are hearing the word which is able to save their souls, do they not frequently find such thoughts as make them afraid lest it should turn to their condemnation, rather than their salvation? Is it not often the same case, while they are endeavouring to offer up their prayers to God, whether in public or private? Nay, while they are engaged in the most solemn service, even while they are at the table of the Lord, what manner of thoughts arise in them! Are not their hearts sometimes wandering to the ends of the earth; sometimes filled with such imaginations, as make them fear lest all their sacrifice should be an abomination to the Lord? So that they are now more ashamed of their best duties, than they were once of their worst sins.

Again: how many *sins of omission* are they chargeable with! We know the words of the Apostle: 'To him that knoweth to do good, and doeth it not, to him it is sin.' But do they not know a thousand instances, wherein they might have done good, to enemies, to strangers, to their brethren, either with regard to their bodies or their souls, and they did it not? How many omissions have they been guilty of, in their duty toward God! How many opportunities of communicating, of hearing His word, of public or private prayer, have they neglected! So great reason had even that holy man. Archbishop Usher, after all his labours for God, to cry out almost with his dying breath, 'Lord, forgive me my sins of omission!'

But besides these outward omissions, may they not find in themselves *inward defects* without number? defects of every kind: they have not the love, the fear, the confidence they ought to have, toward God. They have not the love which is due to their neighbour, to every child of man; no, nor even that which is due to their brethren, to every child of God, whether those that are at a distance from them, or those with whom they are immediately connected. They have no holy temper in the degree they ought;

they are defective in everything—in a deep consciousness of which they are ready to cry out, with M. De Renty, 'I am a ground all overrun with thorns'; or, with Job, 'I am vile: I abhor myself, and repent as in dust and ashes.'

A conviction of their *guiltiness* is another branch of that repentance which belongs to the children of God. But this is cautiously to be understood, and in a peculiar sense. For it is certain, 'there is no condemnation to them that are in Christ Jesus,' that believe in Him, and, in the power of that faith, 'walk not after the flesh, but after the Spirit.' Yet can they no more bear the *strict justice* of God now, than before they believed. This pronounces them to be still *worthy of death*, on all the preceding accounts. And it would absolutely condemn them thereto, were it not for the atoning blood. Therefore they are thoroughly convinced, that they still *deserve* punishment, although it is hereby turned aside from them. But here there are extremes on one hand and on the other, and few steer clear of them. Most men strike on one or the other, either thinking themselves condemned when they are not, or thinking they *deserve* to be acquitted. Nay the truth lies between: they still *deserve*, strictly speaking only the damnation of hell. But what they deserve does not come upon them, because they 'have an Advocate with the Father.' His life, and death, and intercession still interpose between them and condemnation.

A conviction of their *utter helplessness* is yet another branch of this repentance. I mean hereby two things: first, that they are no more able now of *themselves* to think one good thought, to form one good desire, to speak one good word, or do one good work, than before they were justified; that they have still no kind or degree of strength of *their own*; no power either to do good, or resist evil; no ability to conquer or even withstand the world, the devil, or their own evil nature. They can, it is certain, do all these things; but it is not by their own strength. They have power to overcome all these enemies; for 'sin hath no more dominion over them'; but it is not from nature, either in whole or in part; it is the *mere* gift of God: not is it given all at once, as if they had a stock laid up for many years; but from moment to moment.

By this helplessness I mean, secondly, an absolute inability to deliver ourselves from that guiltiness or desert of punishment whereof we are still conscious; yea, and an inability to remove, by all the grace we have (to say nothing of our natural powers), either the pride, self-will, love of the world, anger, and general proneness to depart from God, which we experimentally know to *remain* in the heart, even of them that are regenerate; or the evil which, in spite of all our endeavours, cleaves to all our words and actions. Add to this, an utter inability wholly to avoid uncharitable, and, much more, unprofitable, conversation: and an inability to avoid sins of omission, or to supply the numberless defects we are convinced of; especially the want of love, and other right tempers both to God and man.

If any man is not satisfied of this, if any believes that whoever is justified is able to remove these sins out of his heart and life, let him make the experiment. Let him try whether, by the grace he has already received, he can expel pride, self-will, or inbred sin in general. Let him try whether he can cleanse his words and actions from all mixture of evil; whether he can avoid all uncharitable and unprofitable conversation, with all the sins of omission; and, lastly, whether he can supply the numberless defects which he still finds in himself. Let him not be discouraged by one or two experiments, but repeat the trial again and again; and the longer he tries, the more deeply will he be convinced of his utter helplessness in all these respects.

Indeed this is so evident a truth, that wellnigh all the children of God, scattered abroad, however they differ in other points, yet generally agree in this: that although we may, 'by the Spirit, mortify the deeds of the body,' resist and conquer both outward and inward sin: although we may *weaken* our enemies day by day; yet we cannot *drive them out*. By all the grace which is given at justification we cannot extirpate them. Though we watch and pray ever so much, we cannot wholly cleanse either our hearts or hands. Most sure we cannot, till it shall please our Lord to speak to our hearts again; to speak the second time, 'Be clean'; and then only the leprosy is cleansed. Then only, the evil root, the carnal mind, is destroyed; and inbred sin subsists no more. But if there be no such second change, if there be no instantaneous deliverance after justification, if there be *none but* a gradual work of God (that there is a gradual work none denies), then we must be content, as well as we can, to remain full of sin till death; and, if so, we must remain guilty till death, continually *deserving* punishment. For it is impossible the guilt, or desert of punishment, should be removed from us, as long as all this sin remains in our heart, and cleaves to our words and actions. Nay, in rigorous justice, all we think, and speak, and act, continually increases it.

In this sense we are to *repent*, after we are justified. And till we do so, we can go no farther. For, till we are sensible of our disease, it admits of no cure. But, supposing we do thus repent, then are we called to 'believe the gospel.'

And this also is to be understood in a peculiar sense, different from that wherein we believed in order to justification. Believe the glad tidings of great salvation, which God hath prepared for all people. Believe that He who is 'the brightness of His Father's glory, the express image of His person,' is 'able to save unto the uttermost all that come unto God through Him.' He is able to save you from all the sin that still remains in your heart. He is able to save you from all the sin that cleaves to all your words and actions. He is able to save you from sins of omission, and to supply whatever is wanting in you. It is true, this is impossible with man; but with God-Man all things are possible. For what can be too hard for Him who hath 'all power in heaven and earth'? Indeed, His bare power to do this is not a sufficient foundation for our faith that He will do it, that He will thus exert His power, unless He hath promised it. But this He has done; He has promised it over and over in the strongest terms. He has given us these 'exceeding great and precious promises,' both in the Old and the New Testaments. So we read in the law, in the most ancient part of the oracles of God, 'The Lord thy God will circumcise thy heart, and the heart of thy seed, to love the Lord thy God with all thy heart, and with all thy soul' (Deut. 30:6). So in the Psalms, 'He shall redeem Israel,' the Israel of God, 'from all his sins.' So in the Prophet, 'Then will I sprinkle clean water upon you, and ye shall be clean: from all your filthiness, and from all your idols, will I cleanse you. And I will put My Spirit within you, and ye shall keep My judgements, and do them. I will also save you from all your uncleannesses' (Ezek. 36:25, &c.). So likewise in the New Testament, 'Blessed be the Lord God of Israel; for He hath visited and redeemed His people, and hath raised up an horn of salvation for us . . . to perform the oath which He sware to our father Abraham, that He would grant unto us, that we being delivered out of the hands of our enemies should serve Him without fear, in holiness and righteousness before Him, all the days of our life' (Luke 1:68, &c.).

You have therefore good reason to believe, He is not only able, but willing to do this; to cleanse you from all your filthiness of flesh and spirit; to 'save you from all your uncleannesses.' This is the thing which you now long for; this is the faith which you now particularly need, namely, that the Great Physician, the Lover of my soul, is willing to make me clean. But is He willing to do this to-morrow, or to-day? Let Him answer for Himself: 'To-day, if ye will hear' My 'voice, harden not your hearts.' If you put it off till tomorrow, you harden your hearts; you refuse to hear His voice. Believe, therefore, that He is willing to save you *to-day*. He is willing to save you *now*. 'Behold, now is the accepted time.' He now saith, 'Be thou clean!' Only believe, and you also will immediately find, 'all things are possible to him that believeth.'

Continue to believe in Him that loved thee, and gave Himself for thee; that bore all thy sins in His own body on the tree; and He saveth thee from all condemnation, by His blood continually applied. Thus it is that we continue in a justified state. And when we go on 'from faith to faith,' when we have faith to be cleansed from indwelling sin, to be saved from all our uncleanesses, we are likewise saved from all that *guilt*, that *desert* of punishment, which we felt before. So that then we may say, not only,

> *Every moment, Lord, I want*
> *The merit of Thy death;*

but, likewise, in the full assurance of faith,

> *Every moment, Lord, I have*
> *The merit of Thy death!*

For, by that faith in His life, death, and intercession for us, renewed from moment to moment, we are every whit clean, and there is not only now no condemnation for us, but no such desert of punishment as was before, the Lord cleansing both our hearts and lives.

By the same faith we feel the power of Christ every moment resting upon us, whereby alone we are what we are; whereby we are enabled to continue in spiritual life, and without which, notwithstanding all our present holiness, we should be devils the next moment. But as long as we retain our faith in Him, we 'draw water out of the wells of salvation.' Leaning on our Beloved, even Christ in us the hope of glory, who dwelleth in our hearts by faith, who likewise is ever interceding for us at the right hand of God, we receive help from Him, to think, and speak, and act, what is acceptable in His sight. Thus does He 'prevent' them that believe, in all their 'doings, and further them with His continual help'; so that all their designs, conversations, and actions are 'begun, continued, and ended in Him.' Thus doth He 'cleanse the thoughts of their hearts, by the inspiration of His Holy Spirit, that they may perfectly love Him, and worthily magnify His holy name.'

Thus it is, that in the children of God, repentance and faith exactly answer each other. By repentance we feel the sin remaining in our hearts, and cleaving to our words and actions: by faith, we receive the power of God in Christ, purifying our hearts, and cleansing our hands. By repentance, we are still sensible that we deserve punishment for all our tempers, and words, and actions; by faith, we are conscious that our Advocate with the Father is continually pleading for us, and thereby continually turning aside all condemnation and punishment from us. By repentance we have an abiding conviction that there is no help in us: by faith we receive not only mercy, 'but grace to help in' *every* 'time of need.' Repentance disclaims the very possibility of any other help: faith accepts all the help we stand in need of, from Him that hath all power in heaven and earth. Repentance says, 'Without Him I can do nothing': faith says, 'I can do all things through Christ strenthening me.' Through Him I can not only overcome, but expel, all the enemies of my soul. Through Him I can 'love the Lord my God with all my heart, mind, soul, and strength'; yea, and 'walk in holiness and righteousness before Him all the days of my life.'

From what has been said we may easily learn the mischievousness of that opinion—that we are *wholly* sanctified when we are justified; that our hearts are then cleansed from all sin. It is true, we are then delivered, as was observed before, from the dominion of outward sin; and, at the same time, the power of inward sin is so broken, that we need no longer follow, or be led by it: but it is by no means true, that inward sin is then totally destroyed; that the root of pride, self-will, anger, love of the world, is then taken out of the heart; or that the carnal mind, the heart bent to backsliding, are entirely extirpated. And to suppose the contrary is not, as some may think, an innocent harmless mistake. No: it does immense harm; it entirely blocks up the way to any farther change; for it is manifest, 'they that are whole need not a physician, but they that are sick.' *If*, therefore, we think we are quite made whole already, there is no room to seek any further healing. On this supposition it is absurd to expect a father deliverance from sin, whether gradual or instantaneous.

On the contrary, a deep conviction that we are not yet whole; that our hearts are not fully purified; that there is yet in us a 'carnal mind,' which is still in its nature 'enmity against God'; that a whole body of sin remains in our heart, weakened indeed, but not destroyed; shows, beyond all possibility of doubt, the absolute necessity of a father change. We allow, that at the very moment of justification, we are *born again*: in that instant we experience that inward change from 'darkness into marvellous light'; from the image of the brute and the devil, into the image of God; from the earthly, sensual, devilish mind, to the mind which was in Christ Jesus. But are we then *entirely* changed? Are we *wholly* transformed into the image of Him that created us? Far from it: we still retain a depth of sin; and it is the consciousness of this which constrains us to groan, for a full deliverance, to Him that is mighty to save. Hence it is, that those believers who are not convinced of the deep corruption of their hearts, or but slightly, and, as it were, notionally convinced, have little concern about *entire sanctification*. They may possibly hold the opinion, that such a thing is to be, either at death, or some time they know not when, before it. But they have no great uneasiness for the want of it, and no great hunger or thirst after it. They cannot, until they know themselves better, until they repent in the sense above described, until God unveils the inbred monster's face, and shows them the real state of their souls. Then only, when they feel the burden, will they groan for deliverance from it. Then, and not till then, will they cry out, in the agony of their soul.

> *Break off the yoke of inbred sin,*
> And full set my spirit free!
> I cannot rest till pure within,
> *Till I am wholly lost in Thee.*

We may learn from hence, secondly, that a deep conviction of our *demerit*, after we are accepted (which in one sense may be termed guilt), is absolutely necessary, in order to our seeing the true value of the atoning blood; in order to our feeling that we need this as much, after we are justified, as ever we did before. Without this conviction, we cannot but account the blood of the covenant *as a common thing*, something of which we have not now any great need, seeing all our past sins are blotted out. Yea, but if both our hearts and lives are thus unclean, there is a kind of guilt which we are contracting every moment, and which, of consequence, would every moment expose us to fresh condemnation, but that

> *He ever lives above,*
>   For us to intercede,
> His all atoning love,
>   *His precious blood, to plead.*

It is this repentance, and the faith intimately connected with it, which are expressed in those strong lines—

> *I sin in every breath I draw,*
> Nor do Thy will, nor keep Thy law
>   On earth, as angels do above:
> But still the fountain open stands,
> Washes my feet, my heart, my hands,
>   *Till I am perfected in love.*

We may observe, thirdly, a deep conviction of our utter *helplessness*, of our total inability to retain anything we have received, much more to deliver ourselves from the world of iniquity remaining both in our hearts and lives, teaches us truly to live upon Christ by faith, not only as our Priest, but as our King. Hereby we are brought to 'magnify Him,' indeed; to 'give Him all the glory of His grace'; to 'make Him a whole Christ, an entire Saviour; and truly to set the crown upon His head.' These excellent words, as they have frequently been used, have little or no meaning; but they are fulfilled in a strong and deep sense, when we thus, as it were, go out of ourselves, in order to be swallowed up in Him; when we sink into nothing, that He may be all in all. Then, His almighty grace having abolished 'every high thing which exalted itself against Him; every temper, and thought, and word, and work 'is brought to the obedience of Christ.'

Notes

Notes

Notes

Notes

Notes

Notes

Other *Collection of Classics* Titles